Kwanzaa

by Janet Riehecky
illustrated by Lydia Halverson

created by Wing Park Publishers

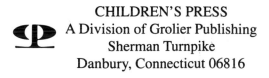
CHILDREN'S PRESS
A Division of Grolier Publishing
Sherman Turnpike
Danbury, Connecticut 06816

Library of Congress Cataloging-in-Publication Data

Riehecky, Janet, 1953-
    Kwanzaa / by Janet Riehecky ; illustrated by Lydia Halverson.
        p.   cm.
    Summary: Introduces Kwanzaa, the holiday in which African
Americans celebrate their cultural heritage.
    ISBN 0-516-00686-X
    1. Kwanzaa—Juvenile literature. [1. Kwanzaa.   2. Afro
-Americans—Social life and customs.]   I. Halverson, Lydia, ill.
II. Title.
GT4403.R54   1993
394.2'68—dc20   93-17076
                                                            CIP
                                                            AC

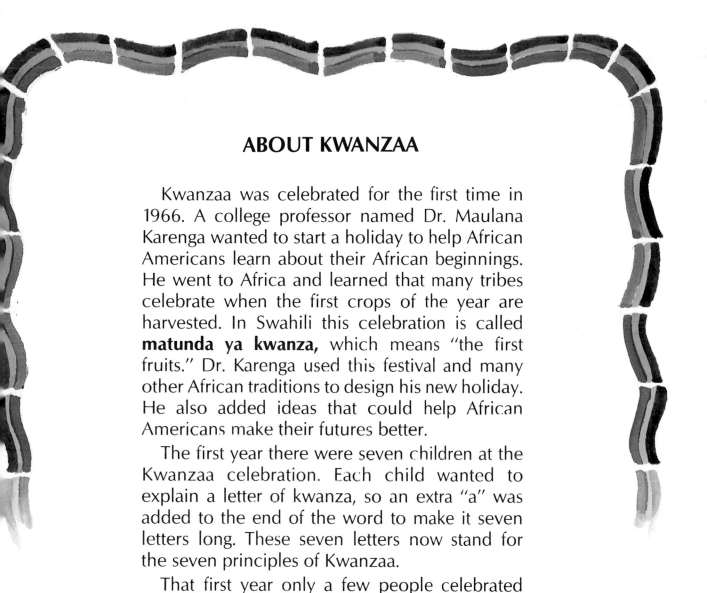

ABOUT KWANZAA

Kwanzaa was celebrated for the first time in 1966. A college professor named Dr. Maulana Karenga wanted to start a holiday to help African Americans learn about their African beginnings. He went to Africa and learned that many tribes celebrate when the first crops of the year are harvested. In Swahili this celebration is called **matunda ya kwanza,** which means "the first fruits." Dr. Karenga used this festival and many other African traditions to design his new holiday. He also added ideas that could help African Americans make their futures better.

The first year there were seven children at the Kwanzaa celebration. Each child wanted to explain a letter of kwanza, so an extra "a" was added to the end of the word to make it seven letters long. These seven letters now stand for the seven principles of Kwanzaa.

That first year only a few people celebrated Kwanzaa. Now more than half a million celebrate each year.

Kwanzaa is an African American holiday. It is a time for fun and celebration. It is also a time for learning. During Kwanzaa, African Americans tell stories. Some tell about things

that have happened in their families. Others tell about great African Americans such as Martin Luther King, Jr. These stories help African Americans to be proud of their people.

Kwanzaa lasts for seven days—from December 26 to January 1. Each day, there is a special idea to think about.

Some families make a poster listing the seven special ideas or beliefs. They use it as a decoration for their home.

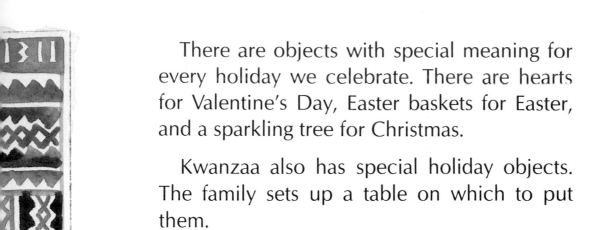

There are objects with special meaning for every holiday we celebrate. There are hearts for Valentine's Day, Easter baskets for Easter, and a sparkling tree for Christmas.

Kwanzaa also has special holiday objects. The family sets up a table on which to put them.

9

The first special object people put on the table is a mkeka (m-KEH-ka), a mat made by hand. The African people have always made things by hand. The mat helps African Americans remember this and be proud.

Next, a large cup called the kikombe cha umoja (kee-KOM-beh chah oo-MO-jah) is put on the mat. Everyone who comes to celebrate takes a drink from the cup. This shows that the African Americans are one people.

Then, a bowl of fruit, called mazao (mah-ZAH-oh), is added. It is to remind everyone that hard work is rewarded.

The fruit is followed by the muhindi (moo-HIN-de), ears of corn. There is one ear for each child in the family. The corn is a reminder that children are the hope of the future.

13

Next to be added is the kinara (ki-NAH-rah), a candleholder. It holds seven candles. There is one black candle. It stands for African Americans. There are three red candles. They are to show how people have to work hard and sometimes fight for freedom. And last, there are three green candles. These stand for hope.

The last items to go on the table are the gifts. In Swahili, gifts are called zawadi (zah-WAH-dee). Some families give gifts every day during Kwanzaa. Others wait until the last day and give them all.

Many people make the gifts by hand or give special things that once belonged to a grandmother or grandfather.

For seven nights, the family meets together. The first night, the black candle is lit. The next night the black and one red candle are lit. One more candle is lit each night until all seven are glowing.

Each night, after the candles are lit, someone in the family explains the idea or belief for that day. Then stories are told to help everyone understand it.

On the sixth night, there is a big feast. It is called karamu (kah-RAH-moo). Special food is made and everyone shares.

Some favorite foods at karamu are baked catfish, collard greens, black-eyed peas and sweet potato pie.

On the last night of Kwanzaa, all seven candles are lit and the children receive their gifts.

Then everyone talks about what they hope will happen in the coming year.

The greeting used during the celebration is "Harambee!" This means, "Let's all pull together." Everyone shouts it together seven times for the seven beliefs of Kwanzaa.

Kwanzaa helps African Americans remember the things they have done in the past.
It also helps them make plans for the future.

But most of all, it helps African Americans be
proud of who they are.

ACTIVITY PAGES

A Mkeka

(Your teacher will help by supplying the materials and showing you how to weave the strips together to make the mkeka.)

A mkeka is usually woven from straw by hand, but you can make one from paper. You will need red, green, and black 18" x 12" construction paper, scissors, and glue.

1. Cut twelve strips of paper eighteen inches long and one inch wide, four each from the different colors.

2. Place them next to each other on a flat surface, alternating the colors.

3. Cut eighteen strips of paper (six each from the different colors) twelve inches long and one inch wide.

4. Glue one twelve-inch strip along the edges of the eighteen-inch strips to hold all the long strips together.

5. Weave in each twelve-inch strip, starting next to the strip you glued on the ends. Go above one strip and then below the next one to the end. Be sure the second strip alternates, going below the strip your first one went above.

Make a Kinara

It is also traditional to make your own kinara. Here's one way to do it.

You will need a piece of wood (any flat piece about a foot long), seven bottle caps, aluminum foil, glue, one black candle, three red candles, and three green candles.

1. Cut seven pieces of aluminum foil, each about six inches square.

2. Place each bottle cap in the center of a piece of aluminum foil to serve as the candle base. Fold the aluminum foil up, but leave it loose to mold to a candle.

3. Glue each cap and foil cover onto the wood in a straight line. (You may wish to decorate the wood first.)

4. After the holders have dried, put the black candle in the center holder, the three red candles in the holders on the left and the three green candles in the holders on the right. Press the aluminum foil around the candles to hold them tight.

A Gift for Mom and Dad

A print of your hand would be a special zawadi you could give your parents. Here's how to make one.

You will need plaster of paris and a plastic lid from a can of coffee.

1. Mix the plaster of paris according to the package directions.

2. Fill the plastic lid with the plaster.

3. Allow the plaster to harden slightly, then press your hand into the plaster carefully and pull your hand up, leaving your print there.

4. Allow the plaster to harden completely, then remove the plastic lid.

5. Write your name and the date on the back of the print.

December 1993

A PARAPHRASE OF THE SEVEN PRINCIPLES LAID DOWN BY DR. MAULANA KARENGA

Umoja (Unity) — To be together as a family, community, nation, and race.

Kujichagulia (Self-Determination) — To decide our own future.

Ujima (Collective Work and Responsibility) — To work together and be responsible for each other.

Ujamaa (Cooperative Economics) — To operate our own stores, shops, and other businesses.

Nia (Purpose) — To do what we can to make our people great.

Kuumba (Creativity) — To do as much as we can to create beautiful and strong communities— to improve our communities.

Imani (Faith) — To believe in ourselves and our people.